GOD
IS IN CONTROL

Marie Rose McIntyre

Marie Rose McIntyre
God is in Control
© 2016
(themarierose@gmail.com)

Anointed Fire House Publishing

ISBN-13: 978-0692727829
ISBN-10: 0692727825

Disclaimer: This book is designed to provide information and motivation to our readers. It is sold with the understanding that the publisher is not engaged to render any type of psychological, legal, or any other kind of professional advice. No warranties or guarantees are expressed or implied by the author, since every man has his own measure of faith. The individual author(s) shall not be liable for any physical, psychological, emotional, financial, or commercial damages, including; but not limited to, special, incidental, consequential or other damages. Our views and rights are the same: You are responsible for your own choices, actions, and results.

This book dedicated to my dear sweet mom,
Audencie Escare, who taught me I could do all
things through Christ Jesus.
Sunrise: September 27, 1939
Sunset: February 10, 2010

Acknowledgments

With special thanks:

To my son, Robert, and my dog, Redd, who
God uses daily to teach me unconditional love.

To my brothers and sisters, nieces and
nephews: I love you.

Table of Contents

Introduction...IX

Chapter 1...
    Successful People are Changing People......1

Chapter 2...
    Evaluate Your Self-Worth....................9

Chapter 3...
    The Power of Thought.......................15

Chapter 4...
    Goals..21

Chapter 5...
    Expectations....................................27

Chapter 6...
    Attitude...31

Chapter 7...
    Gratitude...39

Chapter 8...
    Select Team.....................................45

Chapter 9...
    Physical Appearance.........................53

Chapter 10...
    Fear..59

Chapter 11...
    Real Love..65

Chapter 12...
    Trusting God.....................................75

Introduction

If you have picked up this book, it is likely because you have an interest in the power of God. Maybe, you are curious about God or you are wondering if God is really in control. Whatever your reason for getting this book, let me begin by saying that God is truly in control. Most Christians are aware of the power of God. Some come to this point because they possess a hunger and desire to know Him and His ways. Others may have learned God's power through problems or crises that have driven them to seek His face.

I believe that getting to know God more deeply, growing, changing into better people and having good relationships with one another is a reflection of our faith and belief that God is not only in control of our lives, but He can control everything and everyone around us.

God has designed a path for each one of us if we allow Him into our lives through Christ

Jesus. As we learn and experience that path, we enter His life and He enters into us. This changes our entire existence, behaviors, relationships, careers, and everything else in our lives.

The principles of change and growth are in the Bible. It is in God through Christ Jesus. All of God's promises are yes and amen.

Whatever the question, God is the answer!

Chapter 1

Successful People are Changing People

It is possible that your life can be dramatically changed in just one day. When will the transformation begin? The transformation begins the moment you decide to change. Nothing happens without a decision. Ask yourself this question: What needs changing? Nothing is permanent. Your personality, emotions, and everything about you are constantly changing.

A common way for us to react to change is to change jobs, mates, or friends. People seem to think that if they had the perfect boss, spouse, or house that everything else would be okay. But most people never think of consciously

DETERMINED TO CHANGE

changing themselves.

Just look around, and you'll observe two groups of people: those who are changing and those who are resisting change. Some people even defend themselves against it. Successful people are changing people.

A total determination to change will employ virtually untapped capabilities that most people never utilize. You won't have to be told when that moment of decision happens. You'll know it. You won't even need to speak the words. You'll feel them resonate from deep within your spirit. They will awaken your mind, heart, and soul. Are you ready for that kind of change? The choice is yours.

Make the decision

Do you recall the story that Christ told about the old wine skins? They were inflexible, rigid, and dry with no room for expansion. Many people are that way; they hold on to old ideas and are unwilling to admit when they are wrong. Change demands flexibility, elasticity, and a willingness to exchange old ideas for new ones. We learn how to make decisions by making decisions. Go ahead— see your life transformed.

As you begin a commitment to change, make a decision to change— even if it is wrong. Activating a change in your life is a positive beginning and a sign of progress. The decision itself releases the creativity and energy necessary to determine the strategy for the task ahead. What is important about a mistake is what you discover from it. You can't learn from a mistake that you haven't made.
Jesus honored Peter's decision to walk on the water, knowing that he would sink. But He allowed Peter to fail because it was the key to learning and growing.

Wrong decisions can be corrected, but a

decision that was never made can't be corrected. Only when we are free to fail, are we free to examine, explore, and grow!

Guidance comes only to things that are in motion. A parked car doesn't need direction, but once the motor is running and the wheels begin to turn, you can steer in the direction you want to travel. Once you've made a decision and begin to implement it, you immediately feel the power that comes as you control and guide your car.

Our thoughts trigger our behaviors

No one moves without a decision to move.

If left to circumstances and outside influences, your life would lack direction. It would go on without purpose. That's why it is dangerous to avoid making vital decisions for change. Determine your present location and view it from God's perspective. God doesn't change us so that He can accept us. He accepts us so that He can change us. Once we truly see things as they are, we somehow end up with more of a desire to be transformed.

We are all products of the choices we make. As long as we see ourselves as victims, we remain powerless to change. Don't remain powerless. Victims deny the cognitive faculty to direct their own lives. Albert Bandura, the founder of Social Cognitive Theory, says there are three interrelated factors that direct our lives and they are: thoughts, actions, and surroundings. It is how we process information into thoughts that determines actions. Our thoughts are very important.

Proverbs 23:7 KJV
"For as he thinks in his heart, so is he."

Our thoughts trigger our behaviors. Are you willing to change? Take an inventory of where you are now and where you want to be. Yes, change is risky. Will there be failures? Yes. Will people laugh at your intentions? Of course. Share your thoughts with those who are on

your level of personal growth, but remember
that risk doesn't always lead to ruin and failure
isn't fatal. Detours won't matter if your
compass is fixed on your new destination.

Chapter 2

Evaluate Your Self-Worth

How can we determine what we are worth? Who sets the price on the value of an individual? Most people write their own price tags and manage to grossly underestimate their value because they concentrate on weakness rather than strength. People usually concentrate on failure rather than success. They compare themselves to others. Few people are satisfied with themselves. Poor self-perception is the number one source of depression and lowering one's self-esteem. Healthy, God-created self-esteem is the highest and most positive regard an individual has for self.

Get to know the real you. Know yourself. Only

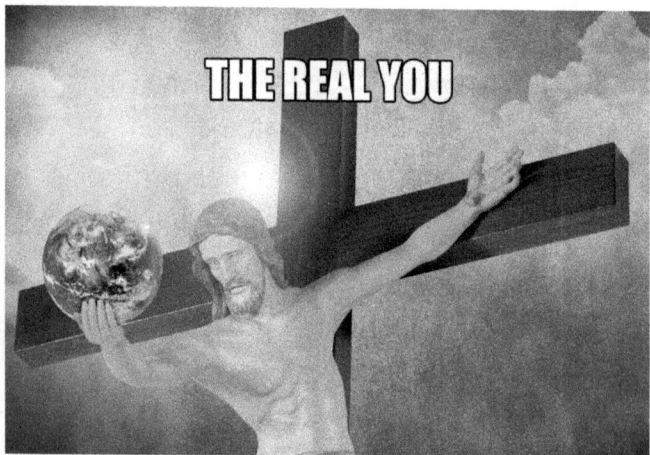
THE REAL YOU

you can come to a conscious inner awareness of who you really are.

Happiness is a manifestation of healthy self-esteem and has often been described as being at peace with one's self. It is vital that you have an honest and clear picture of what is happening on the inside of you.
Laugh often and don't allow personal handicaps to become permanent barriers. Even Jesus had handicaps that could have provided an excuse for failure, but He knew that He belonged to God. This truth more than compensated for any perceived weaknesses He might have felt during His time here on earth.

Love yourself

Our response to failure can result in lifelong negative patterns. Your failures are not worthy of excessive concern and worry. If you haven't failed, you haven't lived.

When the Lord was asked, "What is the greatest commandment?" He answered by saying, "You are to love your neighbor as you love yourself." This means that you must have love for yourself to be able to give love.

Offer your gifts and talents to others who may be in need of them. This can transform your heart and improve your love for yourself. A deliberate, positive change in behavior and actions toward self and others can increase self-confidence and self-perception overnight. Start getting comfortable with compliments. Learn the importance of accepting praise. Many people seem incapable of simply saying "Thank you."

It's equally vital to become comfortable with criticism. Always remember that the words others say about us are not personal until we choose to make them personal.

Avoid saying things like, "I'm not worthy." You have much more to praise about yourself than to condemn. Create a brand new picture; after all, a belief can greatly affect one's behavior. See yourself the way you want to be. Whatever dominates your thinking process will dominate your life, whether it is positive or negative. Think about who created you, and then you will have an idea of your true value.

Chapter 3
The Power of Thought

Most of the time, our behaviors are determined by our perceptions. The focus of our thoughts should be on whatever things are true, whatever things are noble, whatever things are just, whatever things are pure, whatever things are lovely, and whatever things are of good report. **Philippians 4:8 GNB**
Our thoughts contain life and they give life to our health, wealth, and love.

The process of changing your thinking begins when you choose to be confident about the future. Your commitment, hope, and positive thinking provide a strong basis for action. The decision to deliberately choose change instead of continuing with negative, familiar thought

AS A MAN THINKS

patterns and actions may seem difficult at first, but it is well worth the effort. That decision begins with the awareness that you can choose what patterns of thought to accept for your life. It's normal to look at the problem, but we must also be ready to view solutions. Sometimes, it is not so much our thoughts, but our attitudes towards change that determine whether or not our lives change.

For many, negative thoughts result in a state of depression. Depression is a mental condition brought on by what you think about yourself. Consistently negative thought patterns create a powerful misrepresentation of the truth that becomes all too consuming.

Do not be controlled by human nature

Romans 8:6 GNB
"To be controlled by human nature results in death; to be controlled by the spirit results in life and peace."

Your body gives you expression in the physical world, but it is influenced by the content of your mind. In order to live in good health, you must think good thoughts.

Can we truly gain control over our thought life? Can our minds really be managed? We will never experience the changes we so desperately need without a conscious decision to take charge of our thoughts. The "strongholds" that work against us start in our minds and our thoughts. Many people's thought processes are shallow and lead to wrong conclusions. It's time to treat your mind as the treasure it truly is. Starting now, make a decision that you will spend some time every day exercising and expanding your mind to the words and things of God. Oftentimes, a decision to change is provoked when a person feels that he or she is not being led or dealt with in the right manner. This can drive a person into a state of desperation. If we want to change, we must be willing to risk it all, rather than continue to live in our current states.

Chapter 4
Goals

What do you plan to be doing years from today? It is important to look ahead and think about your future. You must be action-oriented and specific about your goals, and you must be as precise as possible. Again, be specific. Make achievable and challenging goals your focal point. Make sure that these are your goals and not someone else's. When it is your goal, your chances for success are greatly improved.

After you have determined your goals, put together a specific plan of action. Ask yourself how you will make them come to pass. Your goals may seldom change, and that's why your plan of action should be flexible as well.

Remember, it is not only about reaching your goals, but the journey to your goals is important. Go through the journey encouraging yourself day after day, exercising and expanding your mind to the Word and things of God.

Believe what God has already done in your life and focus on the potential He has given you. It is not the experiences of your life that determine your outcome; it is the meaning and the belief system you attach to each experience.

By making a deliberate choice to believe and focus on the positive outcome of your goals, you can change your entire outlook on life.

Visualize yourself accomplishing your goals

Visualize yourself accomplishing your goals. A transformation takes place in your mind and your actions when you envision yourself on the other side of success. Make sure that all your goals are in sync with each other. Our ability to envision the final product becomes a powerful tool that enables us to process and transform our experiences into internal models and images that guide future actions. A person with great expectations and beliefs can wake up each day feeling relaxed and ready to achieve their goals!

If you detect a negative pattern of behaviors and reactions to the challenges that present themselves in your life, you have found an area of your life that needs changing. You can drastically change your attitude or thoughts about your life by simply making a conscious choice to do so.

How we experience the outer world is determined by our inner thought world. Research shows that many of our attitudes are developed as adults on the basis of personal experiences. We are not totally the products of our childhoods. We usually do not see the world as it actually is, but the way we perceive it to be. The ability to change your thinking is always in your hand.

Do not make rash decisions

Proverbs 13:20
"He who walks with wise men will become wise also."

When the decision is made to move forward, the chances of success are increased tremendously because of the force and energy behind your decision. Every day, we all face mountains; this is a part of our great expeditions in life. The progress we make achieving our goals can be greatly advanced by those we select to accompany us on our journeys.

The people you turn to for help in this great

adventure we call life can make a big difference in your outcome. How are they influencing you? Are they encouraging you to move forward or are they constantly pulling you down?

You should not make a rash decision to suddenly disassociate yourself from people you realize are stumbling blocks to your future. It is much better to become totally aware of their actions and respond accordingly. My mom used to often say that it is important for us to use "diplomacy."

See people for what they truly are and learn to appreciate both their strengths and their weaknesses. Observe their behaviors so that you can create barriers and detours to avoid any pitfalls that they may create for you. People who have an optimistic outlook on life and who demonstrate personal growth and success in their own lives deliberately create ways to spend more time with such people.

Chapter 5
Expectations

Begin each day with great expectations. Expect each day to be better than the previous one. Negative expectations can sabotage your goals and dreams. Negative expectations can also sabotage your health, wealth, and, happiness.

Expectation is a force that plays a great role in life. Expectation is having faith that whatever it is you are praying or hoping for will come to pass. If you dwell on where you are now, you will not move beyond your present self. When you can see beyond your present self, you can realize your great potential.

People are not responsible for our happiness

EXPECT THE MANIFESTATION

or sadness. We must all personally accept the responsibility for our feelings. Yes, it is true that as humans, we need meaningful encounters of love and acceptance, but we should not forget that the kingdom of God is "within" us because Christ dwells "within" us. We should view ourselves as God views us and not be controlled by others or our circumstances. Your true character and happiness is on the inside. New concepts and fresh information should be as important to you as the air you breathe.

Are you the same today as you were five years ago? Are you hanging around the same people and going to the same places? Who and what are your biggest influences? Whose voice do you hear? Ask yourself this: How can I apply new information to achieve different results?

Take in more than you give out

Expectation believes you have received even

though it may not have yet been manifested in the natural. Thoughts breed expectations and these expectations emit a magnetic force that attracts everything you are believing God for. It is a well-known fact that whatever a person repeats to him or herself, whether true or false, that person will eventually accept as truth. Expect it, believe it, and it will come to pass. Every manifestation was once an expectation. The human mind is constantly attracting vibrations, which harmonize with that which dominates the mind.

Habakkuk 2:2 KJV

"And the Lord answered me, and said, 'write the vision, and make it plain upon tables, that he may run and read it.'"

Mark 11:24 KJV

"Therefore I say unto you, what things so ever ye desire, when ye pray, believe that ye receive them, and ye shall have them."

Chapter 6
Attitude

Does your attitude need a major makeover or just some minor adjustments? How is your attitude towards life? How is your attitude toward your life?

I'm sure you have already determined whether you are an optimist or a pessimist, an introvert or an extrovert, a serious soul or a playful soul. We all know our general tendencies. For some people, expecting negative outcomes is the norm. What is your basic response or attitude to the events that surround you?

Take an inventory of your attitude and the way you respond to people, places and things—especially to issues in your personal life. What

HAVING A GOOD ATTITUDE

is your attitude about these things? If you don't like the crop you're reaping, check the seeds you are planting.

Are your thoughts of love? How are your emotions? Our emotions motivate us to deal with our surroundings and have a lot to do with our attitude. When our emotions are vulnerable, our systems are defenseless. The importance of liberating repressed feelings by looking back at past occurrences and attaching new meanings to them can start a restoration process to our attitude towards our lives and personal situations.

The big picture

If I was to grade your attitude today what type of grade would I give you?

Matthew 5:5-7 GNB

"Happy are those who are humble; happy are those whose greatest desire is to do what God requires; happy are those who are merciful to others."

How can you get a better outlook on life? Here are some things to think about. Don't settle; mediocrity is not a good thing. Start paying close attention to your attitude, your emotions and what meanings you have attached to the things that may be causing a not so favorable attitude. Most importantly, don't justify a bad attitude; acknowledge it, pray about it, and vow to change.

Have you seen the big picture? You should view a change in yourself as an opportunity for you to make a better contribution to the world. Make it your objective to change. Enthusiastic and positive people are what you want to surround yourself with, especially if those traits are not common for you.

Our response to adversity determines our success. How we overcome major setbacks and how we discover light in the darkness are major keys to life and the road to excellence. Excellence begins when we go beyond the call of duty.

High standards in our attitudes

Love has plenty to do with our attitude. What does love look like to you? Love is an action; it is the hands that help. For God so loved the world that He gave His only begotten Son, Jesus, for our transgressions to be paid in full. Love is total forgiveness; it is not holding grudges because of the mistakes of others. Do not keep bringing up the past because doing so only reflects in your attitude towards life. Reminding someone of the past is not true love, nor is it true forgiveness. Our attitude reflects our thinking and what's really going on inside of us.

Most relationships are hindered by past hurts and mistakes that again, have not been truly forgiven or forgotten. True love and forgiveness mean that after you have acknowledged the mistakes and wrongs of others and yourself, that you care enough about your life to let it all go. The ability to maintain your high standards doesn't come easily. It is the result of constantly and intentionally focusing on the positives in life. This keeps our attitudes in check. It is deliberately meditating on what is good in all situations. Keep in mind that excellence is not perfection; it is choosing to stay in the right spirit most of the time.

Our true motives

Knowledge is power; the Bible says we perish due to a lack of knowledge. Never stop growing. The key to a revolution in your mind is to take in more than you give out. The most important book for personal growth and guidance is the Bible.

You can effectively control your day and time by exercising power over the use of your day and the use of your time. Your time is just as valuable as money— if not greater. Time that you've lost or wasted is time that you cannot get back. Use your time wisely and refuse to let others waste it.

Take charge of your day and time. Allow time to work for you, instead of against you. Pay attention to the people and the activities that may be wasting your time and start staying away from them. If you are performing a task for others because you want to get your own way or your needs met, it is clear that your motives are wrong. Are you doing the right things for the wrong reasons? Doing the right things for the wrong reasons can greatly affect your attitude towards life, so be careful.

Proverbs 16:2 GNB
"You may think everything you do is right, but the Lord judges your motives."

A true friend gives without expecting something in return. Questioning what someone has done for you lately is the wrong attitude to have. If you can't help others in their times of need or if you don't have a good attitude or right motives about helping others, it is better that you don't help them at all. After all, God says He loves a cheerful giver. Cheerful is having a good attitude.

Chapter 7
Gratitude

During our seasons of personal change and growth, there is one area in which we can see immediate results. It is the way in which we show appreciation to God and all of those we are around daily. Giving thanks is a vital part of life. God favors people who have an attitude of gratitude. He says in **Psalms 100:4 GNB,** "Enter the temple gates with thanksgiving, go into its courts with praise. Give thanks to him and praise him."

Thanksgiving carries a lot of weight. When God observes an attitude of gratitude in us, it moves Him to bless us. Being grateful and giving thanks is important for our lives. Do you want to experience God's best in all that you could

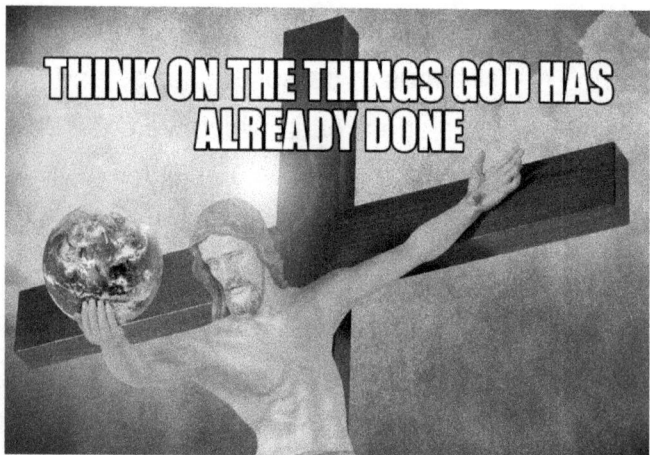
THINK ON THE THINGS GOD HAS ALREADY DONE

ever think or imagine? Start giving thanks.
When you do this, not only will God take
notice, He will do something big in your life and
in the lives of all those around you.

Remind yourself daily about the things that
God has done for you in the past, is doing in
the present and will do in the future. After all,
God is everything we need Him to be and
more.

1Thessalonians 5:18 GNB

"Be thankful in all circumstances. This is what
God wants from you in your life in union with
Christ Jesus."

An attitude of gratitude will deepen your faith
and enhance your prayer life. With the right
attitude, you can walk away from your prayer
time with His peace in your mind and in your
heart.

Being thankful drives out doom and gloom

Do you count your blessings on a regular basis? During your time of gratitude, thank Him for bringing you out of certain situations, the roles of others in your life, for transportation to and from work, for your kids, for your spouse, and even thank Him for your pets. Thank Him for Jesus, thank Him for the Holy Spirit and thank Him for all the things He does daily. Being thankful drives out the doom and gloom attitudes.

After giving God thanks for all He has done, do you seriously think that you can be sad or depressed? Be genuine during this special time of gratitude with God. Don't thank Him just to be going through the motions, but really sit back and think about your day and just start being thankful. Your thanksgiving can be related to something as small as what you had for lunch.

Don't be like the children of Israel. Even though God provided for them time and time again, they were quick to forget about what He had done, and they were very ungrateful. We must be grateful in all things. You have to stay focused on all the things God has done in the past and all He is currently doing.

Psalms136:1- 3 GNB

"Give thanks to the Lord, because he is good; his love is eternal. Give thanks to the greatest of all gods; his love is eternal. Give thanks to the mightiest of all lords; his love is eternal." Give God thanks daily for His mercy and grace.

Give thanks always

Luke 17:11-19 GNB

"As Jesus made his way to Jerusalem, he went along the border between Samaria and galilee. He was going into a village when he was met by ten men suffering from a dreaded skin disease. They stood a distance and shouted, 'Jesus! Master! Take pity on us!' Jesus saw them and said to them, 'Go and let the priest examine you.' On the way they were made clean. When one of them saw that he was healed, he came back, praising God in a loud voice. He threw himself to the ground at Jesus' feet and thanked him. The man was a Samaritan.

Jesus said, 'There were ten men who were healed; where are the other nine? Why is this foreigner the only one who came back to give thanks to God?' And Jesus said to him, 'Get up and go; your faith has made you well.'"

As you can see— gratitude will get us a long way. It will make us well. You can't have an attitude of gratitude without humility. It's a humbling thing to remember what God has done in your life. Humility removes all selfishness. For God resists the proud and gives grace to the humble. God has proven himself faithful. You should get excited just thinking about all of the wonderful things He has done for you. Give God praise, give God the glory and most of all, give God thanks for He deserves it!

Chapter 8
Select Team

In this hour, you are being asked to carefully choose your team. Many people find that they are surrounded by people who aren't genuine in their love or motives. It is sad, but true. A great number of human relationships are conditional. I read an article somewhere that stated that there are two types of people: toxic and nurturing. Toxic people will drain you physically and spiritually. Nurturing people, on the other hand, will encourage your growth. Every time you see or hear from them, they leave you feeling inspired, strengthened, and restored.

Who are the five most powerful people in your life? Reflect on each person and make an

TOXIC PEOPLE WILL DRAIN YOU

assessment of each person's contribution to your life. After your assessment, if you find four out of the five who are beneficial to your life, consider yourself blessed. If you only find one or two people who contribute to your life in a positive way, pray and ask God to bring about the people He wants in your life and ask Him to take the toxic ones away. Begin to focus on your desires for growth and change. Become addicted to a new way of life and new daily activities.

Many people make the mistake of isolating themselves from society when they get tired of being surrounded by negative forces. Seeking out new circles of influence is a better way to go. Results have proven that the most effective way to move forward is to come together with other positive people.

Surround self with quality people

Something extraordinary happens when you

join forces with other positive people. What seems impossible for you to do alone is made simple when it is tackled by a group of people pulling in the same direction. This is why the Bible says to not be unequally yoked with unbelievers. Don't be afraid to ask other good people for help and assistance in your time of need.

The power of encouragement is amazing. The Word of God says to comfort one another and to love one another; it even goes on to tell us to bear one another's burdens. Surround yourself with quality people and remember— like attracts like.

In the past, you may have carried some baggage that attracted the wrong people, but now, you are making important decisions to change in many ways. You will need to have a circle of support that reflects what you want to become— a circle that reflects the new you. The truth is— breaking away from toxic friends and old habits is not easy.

Philippians 4:13 GNB

"I have the strength to face all conditions by the power that Christ gives me."

Old habits and ways are strong; they are ways of keeping you stuck doing the same worn out things with the same worn out people. Take one step at a time. You will never know success in breaking away from old habits and people if you don't first acknowledge that a change needs to take place.

The law of sowing and reaping

Luke 6:31 GNB

"Do for others just what you want them to do for you."

When you help others in need, sooner or later when you need a helping hand, God will send people your way. The law of sowing and reaping is like this— what you do for others will return to you and your loved ones.

Having the willingness to help and treat others with love will help you to develop a new view of yourself and to embrace a change in your attitude. The transformation of self will not only be good for those you come in contact with, but it will also be good for you.

The highest goals in personal success come from those we serve and those we partner with as our support team. Isolating ourselves from suitable people can make the journey stressful and sad at times. I encourage you to get involved in doing things for others and with others. A servant's heart requires and gives love. Desiring credit or points for your well-doing is not the goal; after all, God alone deserves all glory. A key instrument of servitude is seeing yourself as part of a team and that team is God's team. God is the tree and we are the branches. Let us not forget how Jesus picked His team. His team, of course, was His twelve disciples. Remember, later on in His ministry, He took time out to wash His disciples' feet. This is the heart of a true servant.

Chapter 9
Physical Appearance

Our fixation with our physical appearance is not new. You can quickly glance at any magazine cover while in the checkout line at your local supermarket and see just how obsessed we are with our physical appearances.

Instead of following a balanced approach to life, many people are unstable in regards to diet and exercise. New diet trends are introduced each year and if one is not focused, he or she would try a new diet every week. Why do people really diet? Let's examine the most obvious reason— to lose weight. Are you losing weight to be accepted by others? Are you losing weight for approval and belonging?

If your main reason for dieting is to impress others, it is clear that you are bound by the opinions of others. Love thyself as thy neighbor. Love yourself first.

Stop concentrating on others and begin to concentrate on you. End the syndrome of alternating weight loss and gain. When you begin to focus on what you want, you will enhance your perceived personal value and growth, thus allowing change to take place. The better you feel about yourself, the more you will be in control of your needs and your body. Remember, our bodies respond to our thoughts.

When we couple nutrition with biblical concepts for emotional health, we can expect great results.

We have not because we ask not

The Bible says that we have not because we

ask not. How do we remedy not having something? The answer is simple— ask. Ask God for a plan. When God gives you a plan, it will not fail.

Don't follow what the world is doing— one diet after the next and one pill after the next. Simply ask God Almighty for help. Ask yourself what your image communicates about you.

Studies have been conducted to learn how people respond to others based on their clothing. People make instant judgments of you by what you wear. Begin to dress for the job you desire. The goal is not to impress others, but to affect a change in you. Before leaving the house today, ask yourself these two questions: Does my hair look neat and presentable? Is my choice of clothing appropriate for today? Dress for success. When you feel proud and confident with the way you look, it gives you an extra boost of self-esteem, especially if you desire to be more influential and respected.

Make a quick assessment of how your way of dressing compares to the world around you. Let's try something. Pick up a copy of a popular magazine. If you don't have a magazine near you, search the Internet for an online magazine. What are the people wearing? What are their hairstyles like? An awareness of current trends can give you a boost to evaluate self and make changes when changes are necessary.

Chapter 10

Fear

Fear is often described as the most powerful of all negative forces. Fear restricts, inhibits, and causes feelings of uneasiness. Fear works to destroy your faith; it destroys your "can-do" attitude.

2 Timothy 1:7 KJV
"For God hath not given us a spirit of fear; but of power, and love, and of a sound mind."

Memorize the aforementioned scripture. A healthy fear, on the other hand, can serve as a positive force in your life. It is important to know the difference between good fear and bad fear.

A person's thoughts and perceptions of life can

GOD HAS NOT GIVEN US A SPIRIT OF FEAR

be heavily influenced by fear and this inhibits them from moving forward in life. Take control of your thoughts and deliberately focus on having godly outcomes in every area of your life. Choose to concentrate on the results you want and continue envisioning a positive outcome until it manifests itself in your life.
The best way to eliminate fear is to face it and replace it with faith. The Bible says that without faith, it is impossible to please God. Trust God and His promises— have faith in Him.
Let's embrace healthy thoughts and say goodbye to our fears.

Fear is an enemy

Fear is an enemy of everything that is positive in your life. Fear, doubt, and indecision are all cousins; they are all related. Where one is found, the other two are close at hand.

Indecision is the seed of fear. Indecision turns into doubt. When the two come together, they become fear. Before we can master an enemy, we must know its name, habits, and its place of habitation.

Below are seven common fears known to man:
- Fear of poverty
- Fear of criticism
- Fear of ill-health
- Fear of the loss of a loved one
- Fear of death
- Fear of old age
- Fear of change

Keep in mind that fear is nothing but a state of mind. Man cannot create anything that has not first been conceived in his mind.

Again, fear is a state of mind. A state of mind is a mindset that one assumes; it must be created. Fear paralyzes and challenges your faith. If you can imagine something, more than likely, you can achieve it. For this reason, fear attacks our imaginations. Fear leads to discouragement and uncertainty. It encourages procrastination, which, of course, is another deadly force.

Fear leads to sleepless nights and misery

Many people go through life not knowing how fear has affected them. The first step to freedom is acknowledgment. Few people realize or admit that they are bound or have been handicapped because of some form of fear that they have allowed to operate in their lives. It takes a lot of courage for an individual to disclose or admit the presence of fear in their lives.

Below, you will find a list of symptoms to look for.
Indifference: acceptance of whatever life brings without protest.
Worry: to torment self with or suffer from disturbing thoughts.

Doubt: to be uncertain about.

Indecision: can't decide.

Over-caution: the habit of looking for the negative side of every circumstance.

Procrastination: putting something off until a later time or a later date.

Chapter 11
Real Love

Most of us are told at an early age that if we do all the right things, set goals, work hard, and follow the rules of life, we could accomplish great things. What do you say to someone who has done all of these things and more and still hasn't found happiness? What do you say to someone who knows that something is missing, but doesn't quite know what it is? That person has done everything that's been asked of him or her, including graduating at the top of his or her class, obeying all the rules, is responsible, has a great job, has a beautiful family and is still desperately missing something. Most people like this experience a feeling of emptiness that just won't go away.

LOVE WITHOUT CONDITIONS

Real love is missing

You will be surprised to know that there are many who feel the same way. Many are missing the profound happiness that we all hope to find someday.

Half of the marriages in the United States end in divorce. One out of three children is now raised in a single parent home. Ten to twelve percent of us are addicted to something. One-third of all girls and forty-five percent of all boys have had sex by the time they are fifteen years old. Twenty-one percent of ninth graders have had four or more sexual partners. Nine percent of adult males will spend time in jail. Have I gotten your attention yet? These statistics provide an overwhelming view that we are unhappy and looking for something that's missing in our lives. What is missing you may ask? Real love is missing; a love that is unconditional.

Relationships fail every day. The people involved in these failed relationships hardly ever recognize their part in the failure of the relationships. When we do not analyze to see and understand why a relationship may have ended, or in other words, concentrate on our part in the whole ordeal, we are doomed to keep repeating the same things with different people.

Blaming others for our unhappiness

When we are unhappy in our relationships, it is natural for us to blame the other person. We have come to believe that other people are responsible for or determine our happiness. We have learned to justify our anger by pointing out the mistakes of others versus focusing on where we went wrong and how we can make better choices next time. It is wrong to blame the other party for your negative feelings. We blame others for our sadness simply because we don't really know the root cause of our unhappiness, and we need someone to blame. Stop blaming others for how you feel.

Blaming others for our unhappiness is ineffective because it does nothing to help solve the problem. When we are unhappy, it is not the fault of others.

John 4:16-18 GNB

"'Go and call your husband,' Jesus told her 'and come back.' 'I don't have a husband,' she answered. Jesus replied, 'You are right when you say you don't have a husband. You have been married to five men, and the man you live with now is not really your husband. You have told me the truth.'"

No matter how much we may demand others to make us happy, they cannot.

Loving relationships are natural and effortless

When we are unhappy, it is because we are missing an essential ingredient that's important to embrace genuine happiness, and it was missing long before we ever entered into those relationships. That ingredient is unconditional love.

When we learn what true love is and when we embrace it, our unhappiness will disappear. Loving relationships then become natural and effortless.

Most of us have never experienced true love, and as a result, we are unable to make others happy, no matter how hard we may try. Real love is caring about the happiness of someone else without any thought for what we might get for ourselves in return. A love for a pet is a good example. I love my dog Redd without expecting anything in return from him, even though he shows me lots of love and affection. He cannot say thank you, he can't pay any bills, he can't verbally express his love for me, but I know that he loves me. I do for him unconditionally. That's how we should be with the people we are in relationships with.

When we give true love to others, we won't be disappointed, hurt, or angry when they don't show gratitude, are inconsiderate or give us nothing in return. Do onto them as onto God. Our concerns should be for the happiness of others and not necessarily our own. Real love is when others care for our happiness without any concern for themselves. They are not disappointed or angry if we should make foolish mistakes, if we don't do what they want or if we inconvenience them.

Real love is caring for the happiness of others

Real love is unconditionally caring about the happiness of another person. Sadly, few of us have given or received that kind of love. Without genuine love in our lives, we experience a terrible void that we often attempt to fill with sex, food, money, and superficial love. A life without genuine love will always leave us feeling empty, angry, alone, and afraid. Without real love, we can easily become miserable people looking for love in all the wrong places.

Genuine happiness is profound and lasting; it is a sense of peace and fulfillment that deeply satisfies the soul.

John 4:7-10 GNB

"Jesus met a woman at the well who came to draw some water, and Jesus said to her 'Give me a drink of water.' The woman answered, 'You are a Jew, and I am a Samaritan so how can you ask me for a drink of water?' Jesus answered, 'If you only knew what God gives and who it is that is asking you for a drink, you would ask him, and he would give life giving water.'

John 4:13-14 GNB

"Jesus answered, 'Those who drink this water will get thirsty again, but those who drink the water I will give them will never be thirsty again. The water I give them will become in them a spring which will provide them with life giving water and give them eternal life."

Chapter 12
Trusting God

Hebrew 11:6 GNB

"Without faith it is impossible to please God."

If you are struggling to trust God in your life, simply examine your faith. Faith is the most powerful force there is. Faith is a state where you trust God regardless of what you see, hear or feel. Faith is the starting point of all miracles. Faith is to the spirit realm what money is to the natural realm.

Let us start by trusting God in our finances. Have you ever stopped to think what might happen if all of your wishes were to come true? It is possible for wealth to be created for you simply by trusting God for it.

HAVING FAITH IS TRUSTING GOD

Deuteronomy 8:18 GNB

"Remember that it is the Lord your God who gives you the power to become rich but you must first trust him."

Money is important; don't listen to anyone who says otherwise. Additionally, don't listen to the people when they misquote 1 Timothy 6:10, saying that money is the root of all evil. This is not true. The Bible says it is the love of money that is the root of all evil. Loving anything more than the Almighty God is the root of all evil. Money is both an asset and a liability. Many people spend the majority of their waking hours thinking about it, but if we trust God with our finances, we won't have to be part of that group.

Listen to the voice of God

\Money, or the lack of it, has been blamed for breaking up many families and for the collapse of many companies. Would you prefer to make lots of money or be able to sleep at night with

no worries? Trust God with your finances.
The world is divided into the "haves" and the
"have-nots," but as children of the Most High
God, joining forces with our Father makes us a
part of the "haves." Keep in mind that money
only has the value we attach to it. To really
understand the importance and good use of
our finances, we must trust God with them.

I once read about two brothers who were
raised in the same home. When they had
grown up, one of them earned a minimum
wage, but the other earned a six-figure income.
The one who earned minimum wages believed
in himself and his own abilities, but the brother
who earned six figures trusted God with his
finances.

"Money doesn't change men; it merely
unmasks them." ~Henry Ford.

Deuteronomy 28:2 KJV

"And all these blessings shall come on thee,
and overtake thee, if thou shalt hearken unto
the voice of the Lord thy God."

When you trust God with your finances, His blessings will pursue and overtake you. Trusting God will bring you every blessing you dare to believe God for. Once we allowed Jesus to enter in and live in us, we gave God permission to empower us through His Holy Spirit.

Trust God and He will direct your paths

I can tell you personally what it means to trust God. I have been homeless, jobless and without one single person to talk to, but God directed my footsteps and guided me into better days. I ended up getting jobs I didn't have to compete for and cars I didn't have to pay for. Trust God with all you have. Trust God and He will direct your path.

Proverbs 3:6 KJV

"Trusting God is a lifestyle."

To trust God means that you depend on Him

when He's answering your prayers and when you hear nothing at all. It means to believe Him when doors are opening for you and when they remain closed. It means trusting God when you are accepted and trusting Him when you have been rejected. Trusting God is leaning on Him and not your emotions when you are in the process of going through a divorce. It is depending on God to lead your children when they have gone astray. Trust God through it all. When it becomes hard for you to trust in God, remember this: God knows the beginning and the end of a thing; He knows your past and He knows your future. God knows our thoughts before we even have them! The Bible says that God knows every string of hair on our heads (daily).

Matthew 10:30 GNB
Luke 12:7 GNB
"As for you, even the hairs of your head; have all been counted."

All things working together for our good

Trusting God for the changes we want and need for our current circumstances, futures and for our loved ones is what our journeys are all about.

Romans 8:28 GNB

"We know that all things God works for good with those who love him those whom he has called according to his purpose."

Trust God when you pray; He hears your prayers. You can talk to the Almighty God at any time for as long as you want. Isn't that wonderful? Sometimes, you don't have to say a word. Just submit yourself in silence before Him knowing that He hears what's said and unsaid.

Jeremiah 33:3 GNB

"Call to me, and I will answer you; I will tell you wonderful and marvelous things that you know nothing about."

1 Peter 5:7 GNB

"Leave all your worries with him, because he cares for you."

God says that He can make a way out of no way; just trust Him. The God we serve cannot fail. He is waiting for us to trust Him for big and mighty things, and this is all for His glory. Nothing is impossible with God when you trust Him.

Luke 1:37 GNB

"For there is nothing that God cannot do."

It is not what you are going through that counts, but what you are going to— greatness!

Never quit

Let's celebrate! Happiness is inside of you. The purpose of life is for you to grow into the best human being you can be. Change is inevitable, so let us stop resisting it and surrender to life's flow. All obstacles are lessons in disguise;

honor them and learn from them. Your mind creates the reality you experience; learn to make the best of it. Fear will steal your livelihood if you let it; let your faith be bigger than your fears. You must love yourself before you can truly give love or receive love from anyone else.

All relationships are your mirrors and all people are your teachers. True freedom comes from how you respond to life and not from what life does to you. Whatever the question, love is the answer!

James 1:2 GNB

"My brothers and sisters, consider yourself fortunate when all kinds of trials come your way."

You already have everything in you right now to be happy; there is nothing missing that you need to find and replace.

Proverbs 3:5-6 GNB

"Trust in the Lord with all your heart. Never rely on what you think you know. Remember the

Lord in everything you do, and he will show you the right way."

It took me twenty-five years to own my own home, twelve years to publish this book and double the time to obtain my college degree, but God did it! What I am saying is— trust God and never ever quit for **God is in control!**